W9-CEZ-998

PERMACULTURE

Published in the United States of America by Cherry Lake Publishing
Ann Arbor, Michigan
www.cherrylakepublishing.com

Content Adviser: Michael Rockett MS, Natural resources

Reading Adviser: Marla Conn MS, Ed., Literacy specialist, Read-Ability, Inc.

Photo Credits: © Nadezhda Nesterova/Shutterstock.com, cover, 1; © K.Decha/Shutterstock.com, 5; © l i g h t p o e t/
Shutterstock.com, 6; © Nednapa Sopasuntorn/Shutterstock.com, 8; © wavebreakmedia/Shutterstock.com, 10; © AYAphoto/
Shutterstock.com, 13; © Laura Stone/Shutterstock.com, 14; © Theresa Lauria/Shutterstock.com, 15; © Chiswick Chap/
Wikimedia Commons, 16; © Ronnachai Palas/Shutterstock.com, 19; © Syda Productions/Shutterstock.com, 20;
© Ariel Celeste Photography/Shutterstock.com, 22; © TTphoto/Shutterstock.com, 25; © GillianVann/Shutterstock.com, 26;
© O.Bellini/Shutterstock.com, 28

Library of Congress Cataloging-in-Publication Data
Names: Labrecque, Ellen, author. | Labrecque, Ellen.
Global citizens: environmentalism.
Title: Permaculture / Ellen Labrecque.
Description: Ann Arbor [Mich.] : Cherry Lake Publishing, 2017. | Series: Global citizens: environmentalism |
    Includes bibliographical references and index.
Identifiers: LCCN 2016058621| ISBN 9781634728720 (hardcover) | ISBN 9781634729611 (pdf) |
    ISBN 9781534100503 (pbk.) | ISBN 9781534101395 (hosted ebook)
Subjects: LCSH: Permaculture—Juvenile literature.
Classification: LCC S494.5.P47 L33 2017 | DDC 631.5/8—dc23
LC record available at https://lccn.loc.gov/2016058621

Cherry Lake Publishing would like to acknowledge the work of the Partnership for 21st Century Learning.
Please visit www.p21.org for more information.

Printed in the United States of America
Corporate Graphics

ABOUT THE AUTHOR

Ellen Labrecque has written over 100 books for children. She is passionate about being a friend to the environment and taking care of our planet. She lives in Pennsylvania with her husband, Jeff, and her two young "editors," Sam and Juliet. She loves running, hiking, and reading.

TABLE OF CONTENTS

History: Living and Growing Together

Environmentalism is a big word. But its meaning is simple. Practicing environmentalism means being a friend of Earth and all its creatures. Environmentalists want to keep our air healthy, our land clean, and our water fresh. They want to take care of our plants and animals by making sure our planet remains a safe place to live. Some environmentalists focus on encouraging people to stop polluting. Others encourage people to **recycle**. One of the most important environmental jobs is to teach people how all these things work together. Permaculture teaches us that everything is connected. The way we grow and make our food and raise and treat our animals affect our planet.

[21ST CENTURY SKILLS LIBRARY]

Practicing permaculture means learning about where and how our food is grown.

Pesticides can lead to contaminated water and soil.

The Story of Permaculture

Environmentalists David Holmgren and Bill Mollison came up with the idea of permaculture in the 1970s. The word they created is a combination of the words *permanent* and *agriculture*. These two scientists lived on the Australian island of Tasmania. More than 25 percent of Tasmania's land is used for agriculture. Holmgren and Mollison were both concerned that all this land was being used in the wrong way with **unsustainable** farming practices. For instance, farmers were using **pesticides** on their crops. Pesticides help kill insects that eat crops as well as destroy weeds that get in the way of crops growing. But pesticides can be harmful to people and animals. When sprayed onto crops, these chemicals can eventually enter our water sources and contaminate, or ruin, them. Pesticides can make humans and animals sick. It can cause diseases like cancer.

In addition, many Tasmanian farmers were practicing monoculture, or planting just one type of crop. Planting the same crop year after year ruins the soil. When the soil is ruined, the

Raising chickens on an open farm is an example of permaculture in action.

crops become more vulnerable to insects and pests. This means that more pesticides have to be used. Monoculture also means raising one type of animal, like chickens, in crowded barns. These animals are kept in the barns and have no access to the outside. These practices can be harmful to animals and generate a lot of animal waste. This waste can then contaminate our waters, our air, and our land.

Mollison and Holmgren's permaculture ideas were an effort to change all of this. Practicing permaculture means using more natural ways to kill insects and destroy weeds that harm crops.

Developing Questions

People all over the world are eating more meat. Studies show that meat eating is expected to increase by more than 4 percent per person over the next 10 years. What does this data reveal about animal farming? How might the increase in meat consumption harm Earth?

The questions above are meant as think-and-search questions. The answers aren't in the text. Instead, these questions require you to look at different parts of the text and then think about your answer.

Recycling and picking up trash is one way of caring for Earth.

Animals would be cared for more fairly. And water supplies would be protected from harmful chemicals.

These two men began to write books and give lectures about permaculture. They wanted to change the way people lived and farmed not only in Tasmania, but also all over the world.

Permaculture Principles

Mollison and Holmgren came up with 15 permaculture principles, or rules to follow. The three main principles guide us to care for other people, to care for our Earth, and to use only our fair share of resources such as food and water. The remaining 12 principles support these main ideas.

Geography: Permaculture Around the World

Today, permaculture is practiced all over the world. It can be done on a large or small scale. There are several different ways of practicing permaculture. No matter which way you choose, the end result always makes Earth a better place.

Incredible Edible

Pam Warhurst helped start the community Incredible Edible in Todmorden, England. Incredible Edible provides people with healthy food grown right in their own town. Volunteers plant vegetable and herb gardens and fruit trees. They build gardens in places that originally were garbage dumps and parking lots.

Incredible Edible is run by volunteers who care about Earth.

There are over 15,000 community gardens in the United States.

Community gardens provide people with easy access to fresh, healthy fruits and vegetables.

Everybody in Todmorden is allowed to pick these fruits and vegetables for their own meals. Nobody is supposed to take more than they need. Signs in the garden tell people what is growing and when the fruit or vegetable will be ready to be picked.

"Vegetable tourists" come from all over England to see this town. This self-growing practice has now started to pop up in towns all over the world. Anybody can join this movement. Its slogan is: "If you eat, you are in."

Many homes in ecovillages are made from recycled material. This house is made from old barrels.

Ecovillages

Ecovillages are communities around the world that practice permaculture. Some ecovillages include just 50 people. Others can have as many as 2,000. Ecovillages try to grow their own food and create their own water and power sources. One of the coolest ecovillages is the Finca Bellavista Treehouse Community in Costa Rica. It is a community of hand-built tree houses in the Pacific coastal region surrounded by a rainforest filled with wildlife and two whitewater rivers. The community produces 80 percent of its own food and generates its own electricity through water supplies and solar panels.

Gathering and Evaluating Sources

There are many different types of ecovillages around the world. Some ecovillages focus on homegrown and in-season foods. Others focus on recycling and reusing materials. Some communities focus on sharing, including their homes!

Are some ecovillages better than others? Why or why not? Use the Internet and your local library to gather information. Form an opinion based on your findings. Evaluate the data you find to support your argument.

CHAPTER 3

Civics:
Wild Law

Wild laws are human laws that take into account the rights and interests of everything on Earth, not just humans. These laws protect plants, animals, rivers, and all **ecosystems**. Wild laws are the backbone of the permaculture movement. They teach that humans aren't superior to Earth, but rather are part of Earth. This means humans can't keep taking from nature without giving back. Nature deserves a voice, too. Wild laws aren't real laws created by governments. Instead, these laws are a new way of thinking.

Grassroots Movement

Governments aren't in charge of the permaculture movement.

Wild laws remind us to respect Earth.

Grassroots movements inspire people to take action.

It is a **grassroots** movement consisting of groups and individuals trying to make Earth better. Many of the permaculture groups try to grow food locally for their community. Others set up education sites to teach children about taking care of Earth. Maybe you can even start a similar project in your hometown!

Tiny Houses

In order to practice permaculture, people need to live more simply. By living simply, people use less of Earth's **nonrenewable resources**, such as **fossil fuels**. Another way people can live

Developing Claims and Using Evidence

Many people believe it is important to follow wild laws. Why do you think this is important? How would this benefit Earth? Research wild laws using your local library and the Internet. Develop an argument and use the data you find to support it.

This is a tiny house that also uses the sun as a source of energy.

more simply is by living in a tiny house. Tiny houses don't require a lot of energy. You also don't need a lot of materials, like wood, to build one. By living in a smaller house, you'll have more room on your land to grow your own garden and plant your own trees.

Economics: Financial Permaculture

Practicing permaculture doesn't just help the planet. It also helps people look at money and economics differently. People can save more money when they practice permaculture. They can use that money to grow their own food or buy from local farmers instead of from a giant supermarket. When people live in smaller houses, they use less electricity and less power. This means they have more money left over. If people were to bike more, they would not only cause less pollution, but would also save on gas money. The economics of permaculture is also about volunteering your time.

Many people grow their own vegetables right in their backyard.

This is a WWOOF volunteer feeding a baby lamb.

WWOOF

WWOOF stands for the Worldwide Opportunities on Organic Farms. Organic farms don't use pesticides to grow their food. Volunteers can live on these farms and take care of the plants and animals in exchange for a place to stay and food to eat. Most of these farms like volunteers to work six hours a day and do jobs such as weeding, gardening, planting, and feeding, and even milking the animals. It is a great way to see the world while helping support the permaculture lifestyle.

Taking Informed Action

Do you want to get involved with a permaculture way of life but don't know how? There are many different organizations that you can explore. Check them out online. Here are three to help you start your search:

- Children's Permaculture: Take classes on permaculture designed just for kids.
- Permie Kids: Learn about the permaculture life.
- Permaculture Principles: Discover the basics of practicing permaculture.

People buy fair trade products to support fairness.

Fair Trade

People who practice permaculture like to buy things that are fair trade. Fair trade gives people who grow and make things a fair price for their work. Many farmers in poorer countries have to sell their goods at a low price because big companies, like supermarkets or coffee shops, only buy at a low price. These big companies then sell it to the public at a higher price. These people continue to live in poverty, while other people make a lot of money from their goods. But goods, like food and coffee beans, that are labeled "fair trade" means they were bought at a fair price. Buying fair trade means we are giving people around the world a fair share of their resources. Nobody is taking too much.

Communicating Conclusions

Before reading this book, did you know about permaculture? Now that you know more, why do you think this is an important issue? Share your knowledge about permaculture and the importance of helping protect our Earth and all its creatures. Every week, look up different organizations that support permaculture. Share what you learn with friends at school or with family at home.

Think About It

Living a permaculture lifestyle protects our Earth and animals, and keeps us from cutting down trees and polluting our waters. People around the world practice permaculture. But we can still do so much more. Many people might not even know what permaculture is. Why might some farmers not practice permaculture? What factors may stop them from switching to this type of farming? Use the data you find to support your argument.

For More Information

FURTHER READING

Hendy, Jenny. *Gardening Project for Kids*. London: Southwater, 2012.

Spohn, Rebecca. *Ready, Set, Grow! A Kid's Guide to Gardening*. Culver City, CA: Good Year Books, 2007.

Williams, Phil, and Denise Williams. *Farmer Phil's Permaculture*. Pennsylvania: Phil Williams Consulting, 2014.

WEB SITES

Fun Kids
www.funkidslive.com/learn/environment/f-is-for-fairtrade
Learn about the importance of fair trade.

Permaculture Research Institute
http://permaculturenews.org
You can take free permaculture courses online here.

GLOSSARY

ecosystems (EE-koh-sis-tuhmz) all the living things in a place and their relation to their environment

environmentalism (en-vye-ruhn-MEN-tuhl-iz-uhm) working to protect the air, water, animals, and plants from pollution and other harmful things

fossil fuels (FAH-suhl FYOOLZ) oil, coal, and gas formed from the remains of animals and plants that died and decayed millions of years ago

grassroots (GRAS-roots) an idea that begins at a local level

nonrenewable resources (non-rih-NOO-uh-buhl REE-sors-iz) things of value from the earth, like fossil fuels, that cannot be replaced and can be eventually used up

pesticides (PES-tih-sydz) chemical preparations for destroying weeds, plants, and insects

recycle (ree-SYE-kuhl) to break something down in order to make something new from it

unsustainable (uhn-suh-STAY-nuh-buhl) something that cannot be supported or upheld for a long period of time

INDEX

[21ST CENTURY SKILLS LIBRARY]